THE ADVENTURER

THE STORY OF SIR WILLIAM BEESTON OF POSBROOK,
GOVERNOR OF JAMAICA

BRYAN DUNLEAVY

THE ADVENTURER

THE STORY OF SIR WILLIAM BEESTON OF POSBROOK,
GOVERNOR OF JAMAICA

Published by the Titchfield History Society. 2021

ISBN 978-0-993421-34-1

Titchfield History Society

www.titchfieldhistory.co.uk

A catalogue description of this book is available from the British Library

Posbrook

There is not much of an obvious connection between Titchfield and the island of Jamaica, but one young man who was born in the village in 1636 became a pioneering settler on the island and rose to become Governor of Jamaica.

That man was William Beeston, born at Posbrook and baptised at St Peter's Church on 19 November 1636. He was the second son of William Beeston, believed to be a London merchant, and Elizabeth Bromfield, a Titchfield native whose father Arthur was steward for the third earl of Southampton and may also have had business interests in London.

Almost nothing is known about the elder William Beeston. He was evidently a man of substance and may have had some dealings with the earl of Southampton, and there is no doubt that the earl approved the lease for Great Posbrooke house, then a relatively new property, and we must read into this transaction the agency of Arthur Bromfield.

Arthur Bromfield, who became steward for the 3rd earl has an interesting story. He was the second son of William Bromfield of Monkton Farleigh in Wiltshire, and as such did not have much in the way of an inheritance. In fact he received an annual allowance of £6 13s. 4d., and while that was certainly enough for a young single man, it was well short of what a gentleman might need to marry and support a family.

Thus, with little more than his own ability, he entered the service of the Earl of Southampton in 1594 and almost immediately proved himself

A drawing of Great Posbrook Farmhouse

useful by arranging for the safe escape of the earl's friends, the Danvers brothers, who were wanted for murder.

He was loyal to the earl and this cost him his liberty in 1599 when his master was arrested for his part in the Essex plot. Bromfield languished in prison until 1602 when he was granted his freedom on payment of a £40 fine - a heavy penalty at the time. We do not know if he paid the fine himself or whether it was paid by the earl on his behalf.

At any rate, Bromfield was already demonstrating an entrepreneurial spirit and got involved in a number of business ventures. He even partnered the earl by investing in the Fontley iron works and had money to put into the Virginia company. In 1611 he was in a position to help the earl through a loan of £20,000, so it is apparent that he had used his connections and business acumen to build a modest fortune. He also acquired properties in Southampton and London. In 1614 the earl made Bromfield steward of all his estates. He served as MP for Yarmouth IOW on three occasions, in 1604, 1614 and 1621, no doubt acting in his master's interest.

By his first marriage to Lucy Quinby he had a son, Henry and a daughter Elizabeth. Elizabeth Bromfield was baptized at St Peter's in 20 Feb 1605. She married William Beeston no later than July 1628, because a daughter, Elizabeth, was baptised on 5 May 1629. At the moment no place or date of marriage has surfaced but we can say with some confidence that it was not Titchfield. Soon after their marriage, they settled at Great Posbrook House, at the time a newish building.

Elizabeth Beeston gave birth to Henry in 1631, Mary in 1632, Frances in 1633, William in 1636 and Ann in 1638. Only a week after the birth of his last child, the elder William Beeston died. We do not know the elder William Beeston's date of birth, nor his age when he was buried. He may have been an older man and his marriage to Elizabeth Bromfield may have been his second, which leads me to speculate that he may have left whatever property he had to children of a former family. There was no will, which ight lead us to winder if he died unexpectedly He was buried at St Peter's on 3 December 1638.

Elizabeth Beeston, with five small children then remarried to a Dr. Lamb. The record of the date and place of marriage has not been discovered. She was a widow for the second time when she died in 1675 at the age of 70. She was buried at St Peter's on 16 November 1675.

Arthur Bromfield, meanwhile, lived to a very great age. He lived with his family at St Margaret's until 1623, when the third earl appeared to have lost confidence in him. The cause of the falling out is not known, but Bromfield was evicted from St Margaret's and the earl refused to nominate him for his parliamentary seat.

Bromfield was resilient. He acquired the manor of Heywood through marriage to his second wife Mary Oglander. Like many, although there is no evidence that he supported either side in the Civil War, he suffered financial hardship during the 1640s, which were difficult and sometimes litigious. He was probably born at about the same time as the third earl, so he lived a very long life. He mirrored to some degree the enterprise of the first earl of Southampton, although he was much more careful in managing his money. As stated earlier, he started out with little more than some prospects and had to use his intelligence and energy to become a wealthy man. He died on 26 May 1650 and is buried at Boldre in the New Forest.

The same characteristic might be observed in his youngest grandson, William Beeston. William did not know his father who died when he was only two years old and therefore was brought up under the care of his stepfather, Dr. Lamb. We can assume a comfortable upbringing and a good education but all of the Beeston children had to make their own way in the world from a more-or-less standing start.

There is no portrait of Sir William Beeston, but this is a picture of his brother Henry, Warden of New College, Oxford.

The eldest son, Henry, enrolled as a scholar at Winchester College in 1644 and progressed to New College, Oxford, where he was elected a Fellow in 1649. He returned to Winchester to teach and was appointed Master in 1658. He held this position until 1670 when he became Warden of New College, where he remained until his death in 1701.

Jamaica

With two well-connected parents young William started with many advantages. He may have followed his brother to Winchester, but his early life is a blank. Plainly he was not minded to follow in his brother's scholarly footsteps. Apart from the record of his baptism, the first we hear of him is his decision to try his luck in Jamaica as he set sail for the island in April 1660.

Jamaica had been an accidental acquisition. Cromwell had sent out a fleet and a force of 3,000 men from Portsmouth in December 1654 with the intention of seizing the Spanish possessions of Hispaniola and Puerto Rico. The series of Elizabethan adventurers like Drake, Raleigh and Hawkins scuppering Spanish fleets had led to myths that the Spanish were weak and easily beaten. However, sixty or seventy years later, the Spanish were no pushover. The expedition, led by Admiral William Penn and General Robert Venables, first landed at Barbados and then moved to its main target, Hispaniola. There they encountered stiff resistance and inhospitable conditions, and Venables was forced to abandon the invasion. So as not to return empty handed, the force moved on to the smaller island of Jamaica, which at the time was thinly populated and had little economic importance. The Spanish Governor put up little resistance before surrendering. However, the native populations, which included Spanish settlers and African slaves, were not so easily subdued and they retreated to the forest and began a guerrilla campaign against the occupying force. Penn and Venables were forced to return to England where they were immediately imprisoned by Cromwell.

Oliver Cromwell was not a man to give up easily and determined on a settlement policy. 20 acres of land were offered to any settler; it was attractive and demand was strong. Settlers from Barbados, Portuguese Jews who had been expelled from Brazil, and people of various nationalities struggling on the harder land of Hispaniola responded to the call and in five years the island was fully under the control of the English.

It could have ended here but for the restored king Charles II's resolution to keep the territory and establish a civil government under a Governor. In this year the 24 year old William Beeston set out with the risky prospect of making his fortune in this new English possession.

This was the age of the pirates of the Caribbean, a colourful period in history which saw the rise of piracy to a considerable industry. The Spanish had discovered plentiful sources of gold in the New World and had greatly enriched the Spanish treasury throughout the 16th century. Bigger, faster and better armed ships in the 17th century made piracy easier and shipbuilding became a growth industry in England during these decades. The fact that England was at war with Spain gave some legal cover to the 'Pirates of the Caribbean.' In addition, the newly claimed island of Jamaica was centrally and strategically placed for buccaneering adventures in the region. The settlement became a major port.

Port Royal in the 17th Century

Port Royal, as it was now known, was a natural harbour at the end of a sand spit on the south east coast of the island of Jamaica. The Spanish had not bothered to develop a port here, and it is possible that they were already aware of the potential for earthquakes in the area. The English, with no background in the region, were ignorant of such matters and immediately began to build a fort there, named Fort Cromwell. By 1658 there were at least three rows of houses and a church was under construction.

William Beeston encountered a very new settlement in 1660, but the fort was being rebuilt in stone. The community was growing rapidly in these freebooting years. England was in conflict with Spain and was prepared to sanction attacks on ships carrying gold to Spain, thus a group of daring buccaneers established themselves, and not incidentally, the economy of Port Royal. Notable among them was the Welsh farmer, Henry Morgan, who may have been part of the original invading force of 1655, and he demonstrated a great talent for daring raids on ships and Spanish settlements. Most of this booty found its way back to Port Royal where goods found ready purchasers among Port Royal's new merchant class.

One of these was the young William Beeston, who fairly quickly established himself as one of the more prominent men of the community. In 1662 he was elected member for Port Royal in Jamaica's first assembly; the community was beginning to realise that some form of government was necessary and the new assembly was modelled on the English Parliament. Members set about the task of legislating to regulate life in the infant colony. The governor was appointed by the king and was effectively viceroy.

In 1664 Thomas Modyford was appointed governor. He had already made a fortune from as a planter in Barbados and he immediately began to make land grants, principally to poor white Barbadian settlers. They were granted 30 acres each and the sugar cane industry grew rapidly. Something like 300,000 acres were granted under this scheme, about three times the land available on the island of Barbados. Before long, those with resources (Beeston among them) were able to buy out the 30 acre settlers and by 1670 most of the land was in the hands of relatively few planters. 44 planters each held over 1,000 acres and there were 16 who had amassed 2,000 acres or more.

Thus about 60 men held a controlling interest in the affairs of the island. They made recommendations in the assembly; they sat on the benches of the judiciary; they governed the military. Factions naturally emerged, as men interpreted progress only in the light of their own interests. Some clamoured for rapid change; others were more moderate. William Beeston stood on the side of continuing the policy of slow development. The governor was making plenty of money from the buccaneers and was content to turn a blind eye to their activities. Many of the planters, however, began to see the buccaneering trade in conflict with their own, particularly as they depended on safe seas to ship their sugar to London and other ports in Europe. They tried to bring the governor to see things from their point of view and Beeston played a leading part in the assembly's efforts to curb the governor's ambitions. For his part in this protest he was briefly imprisoned. Passions rose amongst those early colonials and one member of the assembly was murdered by another. This gave the Governor an excuse to suspend the assembly and he did not call another during his seven years in government. London appeared to be content to leave Modyford in charge.

The governor further tightened his personal grip on island affairs by replacing office-holders with his friends. Many who lost office returned home unhappily, but, although Beeston was one of those deprived of office, he stuck it out, and prospered as the island economy improved.

Beeston was contemporary with Henry Morgan, the charismatic privateer whose life became romanticised in fiction as a swashbuckling pirate. There is no doubt that Morgan was active in piracy, but the romantic accounts perhaps miss the point that he was an establishment figure whose privateering activities were sanctioned by the British government at the time. Britain was at war with Spain, and this allowed the government in London to privately approve, if not publicly endorse, any attacks on Spanish ships or ports. Morgan made himself a rich man and was able to buy land and property. He was appointed lieutenant-governor of Jamaica on three occasions.

Portrait of Sir Henry Morgan, contemporary of Sir William Beeston.

Morgan was part of the raid on Campeche in Central America by Captain Christopher Myngs in 1663 The raid hauled in some 150,000 gold pieces of eight and made all the raiders, high and low, very well off. Later, Morgan commanded his own ship and made successful raids on Providence island, Portobello and Maracaibo between 1665 and 1669. In 1670-1 he sacked Panama. He was reputed to have gained £70,000 in loot from this

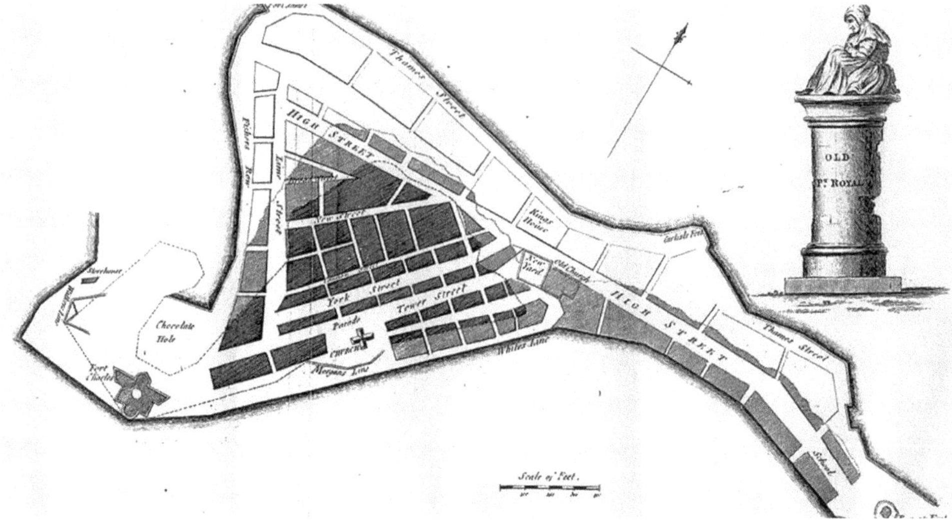

A street plan of Port Royal.

raid.

The political winds changed. Spain and England agreed a treaty in 1671, which meant that England could no longer turn a blind eye to piratical activities. Morgan was brought back to London where he was arrested and spent two years in gaol. Tensions between England and Spain simmered and once again boiled over. In 1675, Morgan was allowed to return to Jamaica with instructions to protect the island.

William Beeston was very much part of this early privateering economy. He may not have participated actively in Morgan's exploits on the Spanish Main, but in Port Royal he was quick to seize all opportunities to make money. He purchased shares in prize vessels, traded in prize goods and island commodities, and from 1662 onwards began to acquire land in the interior. By 1670 he owned 878 acres in St Andrews and had accumulated sufficient resources to begin the expensive work of setting up a sugar plantation.

After the treaty of Madrid in 1670, which promised mutual peace and friendship in America, the privateering and smuggling economy came to an end. Thomas Modyford, who had presided over this quasi-legal economy was recalled and replaced by Thomas Lynch. Beeston quickly adapted and switched from being a supporter of pirates to one who was active in their pursuit and elimination. He was sent to Cartagena after the Madrid treaty, and in December 1670 he was given command of *HMS Assistance* with orders to cruise around Cuba and Hispaniola in pursuit of pirates.

Beeston took a break from island affairs in 1672 when he was ordered to convoy a fleet of merchantmen back to England. War had broken out with the Dutch in that year and shipping was vulnerable. While in England he married Anne Hopegood, a merchant's daughter, on 11 December 1672. The couple returned to Jamaica in 1673, and Beeston resumed business in Port Royal improving his plantations in the country. He also resumed his active role in island politics. He served as member for Port Royal in the assembly of 1673, and each succeeding year, until he left the island in 1680. In 1675 he was appointed a commissioner of the Admiralty court.

There was more change. Charles Howard, first earl of Carlisle, arrived as governor in 1677 with a plan to pass a permanent revenue bill, which would place control solely in the hands of the British government (and therefore the Lieutenant Governor) and deprive the assembly of its revenue raising role. Assembly members naturally resisted their loss of Parliamentary powers and Beeston, who became speaker in that year, was one of the leaders of the opposition. They argued that it was contrary to the government of England 'of which country we [are]' and therefore 'desired to live under those laws.' Lord Carlisle caused further resentment when he sided with Henry Morgan's faction, thus causing some loss to Beeston's business, and that of his fellows. So in 1680 Beeston returned to England with his wife and young daughters to make the case of the assembly to the House of Lords. He successfully lobbied for the return of Lynch as governor, who was reappointed in 1682.

It was probably at this time, no doubt encouraged by his wife, that he resolved to re-settle in England. He had become very prosperous and in 1686 his imports from Jamaica were valued at £2762, equivalent to the income of a large estate in England. In these years, while somewhat adrift from island politics, his business interests were sometimes in peril from a change of regime. Thomas Lynch died in 1684 and the duke of Albemarle, was appointed governor of Jamaica and, on arrival in the island the governor's office was once more allied with Morgan's interests.

Beeston and his associates took advantage of being in England to discredit this Jamaica regime and return the government to one of their own number. Their efforts bore fruit and in September 1692 Beeston was appointed governor and knighted by William III on 30 October. Sir William Beeston set sail for Jamaica in December, arriving on 9 March 1693. He presided over his first council meeting the very next day.

Governor

In one sense he had been lucky. He was absent during the terrible earthquake of 7 June 1692. The earthquake caused a tsunami which overwhelmed most of the spit and much of it sunk into the sea, never to be recovered. Half of Port Royal in fact, constructed at the end of a sand spit,

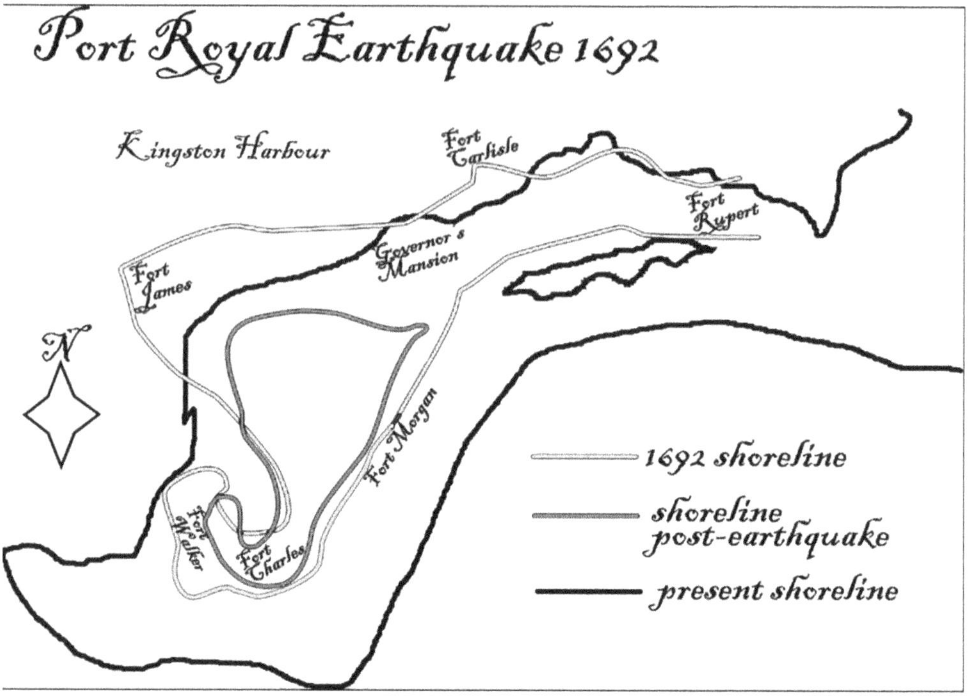

Map illustrating the changing shoreline after 1692.

had vanished, and the governor's house was under water and past recovery. The rump that was left was a small promontory at the tip of the spit. The colony had deteriorated in his absence. He reported that he found Jamaica in a 'mean condition.' Trade had been disrupted since the outbreak of war in 1689. Shipping was in short supply.

Conditions could not have been worse. It was a bad start to his governorship. He reckoned that the damage to his own property had cost him £300 a year. The aftermath of the earthquake may have been more devastating. Severe sickness cost hundreds of lives, and Beeston's own eighteen-year-old daughter, Elizabeth, and a number of his servants died during his first summer back in Jamaica. Hardship drove many more to desert the island, as did the threat of impressment by naval captains stationed at the island. Beeston made repeated complaints about this retrograde practice which harmed the island's recovery. By 1696 he estimated that the island had as few as 1300 white men (over 1000 fewer than a year earlier) and it was intensely vulnerable, not only to French depredations, but to an internal uprising from the 40,000 or so slaves.

Pirates based on the Spanish island of Hispaniola plundered Jamaica's coastal settlements throughout the war causing further economic devastation, and in June 1695 du Casse, the governor of San Domingo, led a major assault on the island. Beeston had some weeks' warning and took steps to improve fortifications and prepare a defence strategy, which was basically to defend a key part of the island and leave other parts undefended. He was criticised at the time, but after a fierce battle, the French finally withdrew at the end of July 1695. Beeston reported that 'they have done themselves no great good but they have done this people and country a spoil that cannot soon be estimated.' The French had killed over 100 people, burned 200 or so houses, destroyed fifty sugar plantations, and carried away over 1200 slaves. Beeston estimated that the destruction had cost the island £30,000.

Communication between these distant colonies and London was slow and news of the potential invasion did not reach London until August, after the French had left. It took time to organise a response and eventually a fleet set sail In the following spring and reached Jamaica in summer 1696. The campaign against Hispaniola was ineffectual. The expedition displayed poor and divided leadership, ill-defined strategy, and resulted in extremely heavy mortality through sickness. Fortunately for the English, their French enemy proved ineffectual, and stalemate prevailed.

Beeston complained of financial hardship throughout his period of office, although this was a very partial judgement. His salary was £1,000 a year, half that of the previous incumbent; however, he had abundant opportunities for profit from his trading activities. In 1698 the assembly voted him a gift of £1,500 towards his wartime expenses, and in 1700 his friend Gilbert Heathcote persuaded the Board of Trade to have him made governor (a promotion from Lieutenant-Governor), with a salary of £2,000 per year. After war ended in late 1697 the island's trade and shipping boomed and Beeston shared in the general prosperity.

He was not always popular as governor. The men he had to deal with were traders and plantation owners with a very direct concern for their own profit and were not inclined to be collegial or always work for the common good. In 1699 his surviving daughter Jane married Sir Thomas Modyford, grandson of his old rival, and in the following year he appointed his son-in-law to the assembly. Beeston put a lot of effort in his later years into trying to pass a permanent revenue bill, identical to the one he had effectively opposed in the 1670s. Such ironies are probably lost on politicians.

Retirement

Beeston became increasingly ill after 1700 and repeatedly asked to be recalled. In 1702 his request was granted and he made his final departure from the island where he had spent most of his adult life and built a substantial fortune. He died soon after his return, on 3 November 1702, and his final resting place was St Peter's, Titchfield. His will left all his property in England and an estate in Jamaica worth £30,000 to his widow, Anne, apart from a bequest of £3,000 to his daughter, Jane, Lady Modyford, who three years earlier had received a dowry of £10,000.

The will was disputed. Lady Beeston, married Sir Charles Orby in 1707, and claimed that her daughter, Lady Modyford, was disinherited after marrying without her parents' consent. She probably meant *her* consent rather than her husband's, who had seemed content with his son-in-law. At any rate, Sir Thomas Modyford was not around to argue as he also died in 1702 and his widow remarried, to Charles Long, in 1703. She and her husband took possession of the Jamaican estate, and proved in this instance that possession was indeed nine-tenths of the law. Lady Beeston pursued a long and expensive court case and received judgement in her favour; however the decision proved impossible to enforce in Jamaica and her daughter and new husband continued to enjoy the revenue from the estate.

In 1698, at the end of Beeston's career, when the colony had been under some sort of governance for a generation, a man called Edward Ward visited Port Royal and recorded these unkind remarks:

> The Dunghill of the Universe, the Refuse of the Whole Creation, the Clippings of the Elements, a shapeless pile of Rubbish confus'ly jumbl'd into an Emblem of Chaos, neglected by omnipotence when he form'd the World into admirable Order. The Nursery of Heaven's Judgements, where the Malignant Seeds of all Pestilence were first gather'd and scatter'd thro' the Regions of the Earth, to Punish Mankind for their Offences. The Place where Pandora fill'd her Box, where Vulcan forg'd Jove's Thunderbolts, and that Phæton, by the rash misguidance of the Sun, scorch'd into a Cinder. The Receptacle of Vagabonds, the Sanctuary of Bankrupts, and a Close-stool for the Purges of our Prisons. As Sickly as a Hospital, as Dangerous as the Plague, as Jet as Hell, and as Wicked as the Devil,

Today we could find a short phrase to say as much, but when Edward Ward wrote his *A Trip to Jamaica*, the fashion was for wordy overstatement. Ports can often be rough places. In former times Liverpool, the east end of London, Portsmouth, Marseilles, New York and Shanghai held such reputations. William Beeston thrived in this environment and turned himself into a very wealthy man.

The other William Beestons

The name Beeston is not as common as Smith or Baker nor as rare as Wriothesley but as a surname it was likely to crop up in various parts of the country. Given the limited range oif Christian names on offer in the 16th century, it must be likely that more than one William Beeston would crop up. The Posbrook William Beeston was a prosperous man who lived in Titchfield towards the end of his life. This would excite no great interest are it not for the fact that John Aubrey wrote that he had been told by William Beeston that William Shakespeare was sometime a schoolmaster in the country. What Aubrey actually wrote was this:

> Though, as Ben Jonson says of him that he had but little Latin and less Greek, he understood Latin pretty well, for he had been in his younger years a schoolmaster in the county - from Mr Beeston.

This man was William Beeston, but not the buccaneering Sir William Beeston, who made a pile of money in Jamaica; he was a well known actor and producer of plays, the son of Christopher Beeston, an actor and colleague of William Shakespeare. This William Beeston was born 1610/11 and died in 1682

Any scrap of information about Shakespeare tends to send the imagination into overdrive and several scholars have been tempted to make the Beeston connection with Titchfield. Is there a connection?

At first glance the connection may rest only on the name. The Titchfield Beestons were, as described above, well-to-do and their sons and daughters would have good opportunities in life without considering the rough and uncertain trade of an actor. Both Henry and Sir William Beeston were able to slide into prestigious positions and need not have given acting a second thought.

Now let us turn to Christopher Beeston. He was a child actor in 1592 and grew up with the theatre. He acted with William Shakespeare in Ben Jonson's play *Every Man in his Humour* and he probably did well enough out of his trade. He had at least one son, the William mentioned by Aubrey, and he died in 1638, coincidentally only a few days after William Beeston of Titchfield. He was probably born c. 1582.

If he was connected to the Titchfield Beestons, his choice of a career on the stage appears unlikely. It was possible to make a living during Shakespeare's lifetime but most families would be very wary of a future for their sons in this trade. The large majority of the actors and playwrights of Shakespeare's day came from modest backgrounds and had little to lose. They were clever men of course and could readily undertake the hack work of putting together a play. Boy-actors, who took the parts of women, were unlikely come from a well-to-do family.

Christopher Beeston doesn't seem to fit.

There is one other William Beeston from this period to consider, a Londoner who weas the deicatee of one of Thomas Nashe's pamphlets. Thomas Nashe, the pamphleteer and sometime playwright, wrote a pamphlet called *Strange News* and dedicated it to William "Apis Lapis" (Latin for Bee-stone). From the text William Apis Lapis emerges as a bon viveur who was not always scrupulous about the way he made money. He may also have fathered illegitimate children.

The dedication is mocking in tone and makes cleare that this William Beestonis the kind of man who did not need to be taken serioously, a character perhaps, good company in an alehouse, but not a pillar of the community. The William Beston of Posbrook was clearly a gentleman and not a person that anyone, let alone Nashe, would subject to ridicule.

All said, even though we know nothing about the William Beston who settlked in Titchfield, we cannot make any connection with any other William Beestons of the period.

The Beestons of Cheshire

A more likely connection may be with the Beeston gamily of Cheshire. Beeston Caste, perched on top of a rocky outcrop near the village of that name, was the family seat of an ancient family who took the name of the village. Sir George Beeston (1520-1601) was a soldier and sailor and was noted for his part in defending England against the Spanish Armada in 1588. On record he had one son, Hugh, who became his heir. The name William does not appear as a son of Sir George.

The only connection that can be drawn between the Cheshire Beestons and William Bereston of Titchfield is that the latter was said to have used the coat of arms of the Cheshire Beestons. This is the recollection of Henry Beeston, who was only seven years old at the time of his father's death.

This amounts to hearsay rather than evidence. We can speculate that William Beeston may have been a younger son of Sir George Beeston or perhaps even an illegitimate son. Either way, the William Beeston who fetched up in Posbrook House was certainly classed as a gentleman and the careers of his two sons would support that theory.

The Titchfield Papers

is planned as a series of brief articles about highlights of Titchfield's history. The list below outlines the planned series. More titles will be forthcoming.

1 The Adventurer: The Life of Sir William Beeston, Governor of Jamaica.
2 A Tale of Revenge and Murder: The true story that inspired Romeo and Juliet.
3 The New River: The mysterious origins of Titchfield's canal.
4 Titchfield Abbey: A history of 300 years.
5 Doctors and Surgeons: A history of medical practice in Titchfield up to the present day.
6 St Margaret's Priory: The full story of one house and its residents.
7 Place House: A great Tudor mansion.
8 Lodgings and Ale: The story of Titchfield's inns and breweries from medieval times.
9 The Founder of a Dynasty: The remarkable rise to fortune of the 1st Earl of Southampton.
10 The Unhappy Earl: The short and furious life of the second earl of Southampton.
11 Patron of Shakespeare and Virginia: The life and activities of the third Earl of Southampton.
12 The Statesman: Thomas Wriothesley, 4th Earl of Southampton.
13 The Great Barn: A medieval legacy.
14 Ghost Stories: A collection of ghost stories from Titchfield.
15 St Wilfrid's Legacy: The history of St Peter's Church, founded in the seventh century.
16 A History of Titchfield Mill
17 The Wriothesley Women: The neglected stories of the wives and daughters of the earls of Southampton.
18. A Royal Wedding: The marriage of Henry VI and Margaret of Anjou at Titchfield in 1445.

CPSIA information can be obtained
at www.ICGtesting.com
Printed in the USA
LVHW072010050122
707933LV00015B/532